cutest ever toddler knits

cutest ever toddler knits

VAL PIERCE

NEW
HOLLAND

First published in 2013 by New Holland Publishers
London Cape Town Sydney Auckland
www.newhollandpublishers.com

Garfield House
86–88 Edgware Road
London W2 2EA, UK

Wembley Square,
First Floor
Solan Road Gardens,
Cape Town 8001
South Africa

Unit 1, 66 Gibbes Street
Chatswood
New South Wales 2067
Australia

218 Lake Road
Northcote
Auckland
New Zealand

10 9 8 7 6 5 4 3 2 1

A record of this book is available at the British Library

ISBN 978 1 78009 100 6

Publisher: Lliane Clarke
Project Editor: Simona Hill
Designer: Tracy Loughlin
Photographer: Graham Gillies
Production Manager: Olga Dementiev
Printed and bound Toppan Leefung (China) Ltd

Contents

Introduction

Knitting is growing in popularity and there has been a resurgence of interest in this delightful craft. There is something very rewarding about creating a garment for someone special in your life and it's even more pleasing to see the garment being worn.

The once staid image of knitting has gone forever, Manufacturer's now tempt us with desirable collections of fashionable and thoroughly wearable patterns and mouthwatering selections of softly textured yarns. In fact, the range of yarns available is mind-blowing with new textures, finishes, and eco friendly products being added to collections yearly. The colours are stunning, ranging from the most delicate pastels to zingy tones that dazzle, making the choice you have when deciding which yarn to use for a project an absolute pleasure.

Having already designed projects for tiny babies in my previous book I have now created a special collection of projects to fit toddlers. These pretty and practical designs for girls and boys will keep them warm and cosy while they play. There are also some extra-special projects for days out ranging from a gorgeous Scandinavian outfit with matching bobble hat and a shawl-collared sweater. For fashion-conscious little girls there's a soft lacy beanie with matching fingerless gloves and a plaited hairband complete with bow.

As well as clothes there are some very cute play toys including a fabulous fish and a sweet play bag complete with smiley-faced fruit. All the patterns are rated according to level of difficulty and range from beginner right through to the more experienced knitter. I have added tips and a techniques section to help you so whatever your skill level and experience there will be a project suitable.

Happy Knitting

Materials and Accessories

YARNS

It can be quite daunting for a new knitter to decide which yarns to use for a project. All the projects in the book have specified yarns but you can substitute these for different yarns. Just make sure you keep to the same ply or weight recommended in the pattern and knit a tension square to check that your choice of yarn will turn out to the same dimensions as the one specified. Increase your needle size if your tension is tight. Decrease your needle size if your tension is loose. If you do decide to change yarns then it is possible that you will achieve a different look to your finished garment than that of the design.

ACCESSORIES

A few basic tools are essential for knitters. Invest in some good-quality needles since these will give you many years of service. A tape measure, stitch holders, row markers, cable needle, a good quality sharp pair of needlework scissors and wool needles are recommended too. A knitting bag is also a very handy thing in which to store your work in progress; not only does it keep it clean while you are knitting, you can store the patterns and yarns you are using all in one place ready to begin work.

Techniques

CASTING ON AND OFF

Make sure that your cast on and cast off stitches remain elastic by either working them reasonably loosely or using a larger size needle than stated if you think you work very tightly. As a general rule most casting off is done with the right side of the work facing.

KNIT AND PURL STITCHES

To create any fabric when beginning to knit there are two knitting stitches that need to be mastered. The knit stitch forms a ridged fabric known as garter stitch and can be used for many projects. The second stitch needed is a purl stitch which, when teamed with the knit stitch, creates stocking stitch; this fabric is smooth on the right side and ridged on the wrong side. These two stitches can be used to work many beautiful patterns and decorative stitches and are the basis for all knitting.

A moss stitch pattern is created by alternating 1 knit stitch and 1 purl stitch on every row. The purl stitch is worked over the knitted stitch on

the subsequent row.

INCREASING AND DECREASING

When working on some projects it is necessary to shape the pieces as you work. In order to do this you will need to lose or gain stitches on the rows as you knit. This is done by either increasing the number of stitches (done by knitting twice into the same stitch), or decreasing (achieved by knitting two stitches together).

WORKING WITH TWO COLOURS

A couple of the designs in the book use more than one colour in a row. When working these it is advisable to use the stranding method whereby you carry the yarn not in use fairly loosely across the back of the work as you knit. The yarn can be tied into the work on every third of fourth stitch to keep it neat and elastic. Care must be taken not to pull yarn too tightly when doing this otherwise it will result in puckering of the fabric.

WORKING FROM A CHART

Charts are read from bottom to top and usually from right to left. The first stitch of a chart is the bottom one on the right. Placing a straight edge of some kind under each row will help you keep your place in the chart when working the design.

INTARSIA

This is another method of adding colour to your work, and is for the more experienced knitter. The motif or patterning is usually written onto a chart for you to follow row by row and the yarns used are not taken across the back of the work as in stranding, but each individual area of colour is knitted using a separate piece of yarn. Winding small lengths of colour onto bobbins or small pieces of card helps to eliminate tangling when using different colours in the same row.

TENSION

Tension is very often overlooked and can have a detrimental effect to your finished garments. Always check your tension before you begin working, changing needle sizes to obtain the stated stitch count if needed. Remember, if you get fewer stitches to the centimetre (inch) than stated your tension is too loose and a smaller needle is required. If you get more stitches to the centimetre (inch) than stated your tension is too tight and a larger needle will be required. When measuring your tension don't stretch the work out to make it fit or vice versa; knit up one or two samples until you get it just right.

MEASUREMENTS AND MEASURING

Most of the garments within this book are designed so that there will be an allowance for comfortable fit. When measuring pieces of knitting while working on your project it is much easier and more reliable to count the number of rows you have knitted. Sleeves and side seams will all sew up and fit so much better if the rows are the same. Sewing in sleeves sometimes causes problems, but if you pin and ease the sleeve in place before stitching you should get a good result. Raglan sleeves are easier to stitch in since they lay flat when sewing.

MAKING TASSELS

Cut a piece of card to the required tassel length and wind yarn around it to the desired thickness. Thread a piece of yarn through the wound thread and tie to hold the threads together. This forms the top of the tassel and the yarn is used to attach the tassel to your project. Slide off the card. Take a longer length of thread and wind around the threads to form the neck of the tassel. Knot the ends, Cut the other side of the loops. .

MAKING POMPOMS

Cut two circles of cardboard the diameter of the required finished pompom plus 6 mm (¼ in) for trimming. Carefully cut out a round hole in the centre, a quarter of the diamter of the finished pompom. Wind wool around the cardboard and until the centre hole is full. Place the point of the pair of scissors between the two pieces of cardboard and cut around, keeping the scissors between the two circles of card all the time. Using a double strand of wool, wrap the threads between the two circles of cardboard, knot firmly, and take away cardboard. Trim to shape.

MAKING UP

After completing your work you will need to sew the pieces together. Sewing the pieces together is sometimes daunting to novice knitters but if you work methodically and carefully you will find it is quite simple. Back stitch gives a neat little ridge on the inside of the work. You can also work from the front of the knitting, laying the pieces to be sewn up on a flat surface so that you can catch adjacent stitches together, one from each piece as you sew. This is tricky to begin with but once the technique is mastered it gives an almost invisible seam, and makes matching patterns and stripes a lot easier. Take care to stretch front bands slightly when sewing them on as this gives a firmer and more professional finish to cardigans. Most patterns will give instructions on making up a particular garment for you to follow.

Always read the ball band of the yarn you have used, since this will give you details about pressing and washing your garment.

PICKING UP STITCHES

It takes a lot of practice to perfect this

technique but here are a few ideas to help. Work through the complete stitch, using both strands, lifting just one strand will result in a hole in your work. Always pick up the amount of stitches recommended, and make sure they are even on both sides of the neck and front. Measure the length of fronts of cardigans, then divide the amount of stitches you need to pick up into the length, that way you will end up with a neat even button or buttonhole band that sits flat. Work through the same stitch all the way up the fronts and always start 1 stitch in from the edge.

STRANDING YARNS FOR FAIRISLE

Some of the designs in this book need the yarn not in use to be stranded across the back of the work. The spare yarn is carried across the back of the fabric, tying it in every third or fourth stitch. It is very easy to pull the spare yarn too tightly which will pucker the work, or leave it too loose which results in large uneven stitches. Weaving in the yarns will give a more dense and solid appearance to the fabric.

CABLES

Cables create an attractive and raised effect to the work. They are very easy to work and just entail slipping the stated amount of stitches off the main needle onto a special short cable pin. This small pin is then either taken to the front or back of the work and left while another quantity of stitches are worked from the main needle. You then return to the stitches on the cable pin and work across them in the normal way.

ADDING EXTRA LENGTH

It is quite easy to add extra length to stocking stitch designs just by knitting a few extra rows before the start of the armhole shaping. However, where patterns, and especially fairisle patterns, are used then adding extra rows is quite difficult since it will throw out the pattern sequences in the designs. Adding extra length to sleeves works on the same principle. If there are stripes on a design then make sure that you end both the sleeve length and the side seam length on the same colour and row of the stripe to maintain the continuity of the pattern.

ABBREVIATIONS

beg beginning

dec decrease by working 2 stitches together

inc increase by working into front and back of stitch

foll following

k knit

p purl

k2tog knit 2 stitches together, decreasing a stitch

M1 make a stitch by picking up horizontal loop lying before next stitch and working into back of it

psso pass slipped stitch over

p2tog purl 2 stitches together, decreasing a stitch

rem remain(ing)

RS right side

sl1 slip 1

st(s) stitch(es)

st st stocking stitch

tbl through back of loops

tog together

WS wrong side

yfrn yarn in front and round needle

yfwd yarn forward

yrn yarn round needle

NEEDLES SIZE CONVERSIONS

Metric (mm)	UK	US
2 mm	14	0
2¼ mm	13	1
2¾ mm	12	2
3 mm	11	2/3
3¼ mm	10	3
3¾ mm	9	5
4 mm	8	6
4½ mm	7	7
5 mm	6	8
5½ mm	5	9
6 mm	4	10
6½ mm	3	10½
7 mm	2	10½
7½ mm	1	11

YARN CONVERSIONS

UK/Australia	US
1 ply	lace weight
2 ply	baby
3 ply	fingering
4 ply	sport weight
8 ply, double knit, dk	worsted weight
10 ply, Aran	fisherman or medium
12 ply, chunky	bulky

Sweetheart Sweater

Knit a pretty sweater for the little sweetheart in your life. The soft sweater has buttons at the back of the neck so it's easy to get over a child's head. The stitches used are very simple; the heart on the front is knitted using the Intarsia method, which requires you to use separate balls of yarn when working the motif instead of weaving the yarns across the back of the work.

✳✳ Intermediate

To fit 2–3 years old

MEASUREMENTS
Chest 61 cm (24 in);
length from back neck 37 cm (14 in);
sleeve length 20cm (8 in)

MATERIALS
◆ Sublime Baby Cashmere merino silk DK
◆ 1 x 50 g ball deep pink (DP), shade 126;
◆ 5 x 50 g balls cream (C), shade 3
◆ 3 small flower buttons and matching thread
◆ Knitting needles size 3.25, 3.75 and 4 mm
   (UK 8, 9 and 10 / US 4, 5 and 6)
◆ Stitch holders

TENSION
22 sts x 28 rows st st measures 10 cm (4 in) square, when knitted using 4 mm (UK 8 / US 6) knitting needles

SPECIAL ABBREVIATIONS
MS = Moss stitch (US seed stitch)

FRONT

Using 3.75 mm (UK 9 / US 5) knitting needles and cream, cast on 67 sts. Work 10 rows in MS (moss stitch). Change to 4 mm (UK 8 / US 6) knitting needles.

Row 1: (RS) MS10, knit to last 10 sts, MS10.

Row 2: MS10, purl to last 10 sts, MS10. Repeat the last 2 rows 6 times more, (14 rows in all). Now work across all stitches in st st for another 10 rows beginning with a knit row and ending with a purl row

Motif

Motif is worked from chart, using intarsia method, over 27 sts reading rows from right to left.

Row 1: K20, (p1, k1) 13 times, p1, k20. Continue working from chart until row 32 is complete.

Continue in st st and cream until work measures 20 cm (8 in) or required length.

Shape Sleeves

Cast off 2 sts at the beginning of the next 2 rows.

Next row: K2, k2tog, knit to last 4 sts, sl1,

0 = purl, / = knit, X = contrast yarn

Knit from right to left

k1, psso, k2.

Next row. Purl.

Continue as for last 2 rows until you have 33 sts on the needle, end with RS facing for next row.

Shape Neck

K2, k2tog, k6. Turn and work on this side first.

Next row: P2tog, purl to end.
Next row: K2, k2tog, k2, k2tog.
Next row: P2tog, purl to end.
Next row: K2, k3tog.
Next row: P2tog, p1.
Next row: K2tog, fasten off.

With RS facing, slip centre 13 sts onto a stitch holder for front neck. Rejoin yarn to neck edge of remaining sts, knit to last 4 sts, sl1, k1, psso, k2. Complete to match first side, reversing all shapings.

BACK
Using 3.75 mm (UK 9 / US 5) knitting needles and cream, cast on 67 sts.
Work 10 rows in MS.
Change to 4 mm (UK 8 / US 6) knitting needles.
Row 1: (RS) MS 10, knit to last 10 sts, MS 10.
Row 2: MS 10, purl to last 10 sts, MS 10.
Repeat the last 2 rows 6 times more (14 rows in all).
Now work across all stitches in st st until back length matches front up to beginning of raglan shaping, ending with a purl row.

Shape Sleeves
Cast off 2 sts at the beginning of the next 2 rows.
Next row: K2, k2tog, knit to last 4 sts, sl1, k1, psso, k2.
Next row: Purl.
Continue decreasing as set until you have 47 sts on needle, ending with a purl row.

Divide for Back Opening
Next row: (RS) k2, k2tog, k18. Turn and work on this side first.
Next row: Purl.
Continue to dec as before until you have 11 sts, ending with a purl row. Cast off.
With RS facing rejoin yarn to remaining stitches, cast off next 3 sts, knit to last 4 sts, sl1, k1, psso, k2.
Complete to match first side, reversing all shapings.

LEFT SLEEVE
Using 3.25 mm (UK 10 / US 4) knitting needles and cream, cast on 37 sts.
Work in MS for 10 rows.

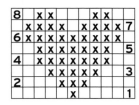

X = contrast yarn

Change to 4 mm (UK 8 / US 6) knitting needles.

Row 11: K2, inc 1, knit to last 3 sts, inc 1, k2.

Continue in st st and increase as row 11 on every 4th row following until you have 47 sts on the needles. End with a purl row. Place heart. Continue to inc on every 4th row as before, taking the yarn across the back of the fabric for this motif.

Row 1: K23 cream, k1 deep pink, k23 cream.

Complete heart and then continue in cream only, increasing until there are 59 sts on the needle. Continue in st st until work measures 20 cm (8 in) or required length, ending with a purl row.

Shape Sleeves

Cast off 2 sts at the beginning of the next 2 rows.

Next row: K2, k2tog, knit to last 4 sts, sl1,

k1, psso, k2.

Next row: Purl

Repeat as for last 2 rows until 19 sts remain.

Purl 1 row. (RS facing for next row.)

Next row: Dec 1 st at each end of next row, then cast off 4 sts at beginning of following row.

Next row: Dec 1 st at beginning of next row.

Next row: Cast off 6 sts at beginning of next row.

Cast off remaining 6 sts.

RIGHT SLEEVE

Using cream and 3.25 mm (UK 10/ US 4) needles cast on 37 sts.

Work in MS for 10 rows.

Change to 4 mm (UK 8 / US 6) knitting needles.

Row 11: K2, inc 1, knit to last 3 sts, inc 1, k2.

Continue in st st and increase as row 1 on every 4th row following until there are 59 sts.

Continue in st st until work measures 20 cm (8 in) or required length, ending on a purl row.

Shape Raglans

Cast off 2 sts at the beginning of the next 2 rows.

Next row: K2, k2tog, knit to last 4 sts, sl1, k1, psso, k2.

Next row: Purl

Continue to decrease as on last 2 rows until 19 sts remain.

Purl 1 row.

Next row: Cast off 5 sts at beg and dec 1 st at end of next row.

Work 1 row.

Next row: Cast off 6 sts at beg and dec 1 st at end of next row.

Work 1 row. Cast off remaining 6 sts.

To Make Up

Sew in all yarn ends. Press each item. Join the raglan seams with a flat seam.

BUTTON BORDER

With RS facing, using 3.25 mm (UK 10/ US 4) needles and cream, starting at neck edge, pick up and k19 sts along the back opening. Work 5 rows MS. Cast off.

BUTTONHOLE BORDER

With RS facing, using 3.25 mm (UK 10/ US 4) knitting needles and cream, and starting at base of opening pick up and knit 19 sts. Work 1 row in MS.

Next row: Work 5 sts. [Work next 2 sts tog, yfwd, k5] repeat once.

Work 3 more rows MS, cast off.

NECK BORDER

With RS facing, and 3.25 mm (UK 10 / US 4) knitting needles and cream, beginning at cast-off edge of borders, pick up and knit

12 sts from left back, 16 sts from sleeve, 23 sts from front (including sts on holder for neck front) 16 sts from second sleeve, and 12 sts from right back (79 sts).

Work 1 row MS.

Next row: Work 1 st, work 2tog, yfwd, work in pattern to end.

Now work another 3 rows in MS. Cast off. Join side and sleeve seams neatly. Place buttonhole border over button border and sew neatly in place to cast off sts at base of opening. Sew on buttons.

Mock Cable Scarf

A simple but attractive mock cable stitch pattern adds interest to a warm, snuggly scarf. Add a fringed tassel to each end to complete the look.
This scarf is made in a soft pure wool, tweed-effect yarn in aran weight, but you could substitute any similar weight yarn, if wished.

✳✳ Intermediate

MEASUREMENTS

15 x 92 cm (6 x 36 in)

MATERIALS

- 3 x 50g balls Rowan Felted Tweed Aran shade 733
- Knitting needles size 5 mm (UK 6 / US 8)
- Cable needle and wool needle

Tension is not critical on this piece

SPECIAL ABBREVIATION

CR3 = Slip next st onto cable needle and leave at front of work, knit next 2 sts, then knit st on cable needle.

Using 5 mm (UK 6 / US 8) needles cast on 32 sts.
Row 1: (RS) P2 *k3, p2*, rep to end.
Row 2: K2, *p1, k1, p1, k2* rep from * to * to end.
Rows 3-8: Rep last 2 rows 3 more times.
Row 9: P2, *CR3, p2* rep from * to * to end.
Row 10: *As row 2.**
Repeat from ** to ** until piece measures 92 cm (36 in) ending on a WS row.
Cast off in pattern.

To Make Up

Sew in yarn ends. Thread a needle with matching yarn, gather up each short end of the scarf.
Make and sew a tassel to each end.

To Make Tassels

Wind a long length of yarn around a 15 cm (6 in) wide piece of stiff card. Remove carefully from the card and tie the threads tightly together in one place. Cut the yarn opposite the tie. Fold yarn bundle in half and tie another piece of yarn tightly around the bundle a little way down from the original tie to form the tassel head. Sew a tassel to each gathered end of the scarf. Trim to tidy.

Unisex Cardigan

An easy four-row yoke pattern makes this otherwise plain cardigan a little bit different. Stocking stitch is used for the sleeves and the main body pieces and a neat ridged twist pattern accentuates the back and front yokes. I used a neutral shade to suit a boy or girl - just change the side the buttons appear on.

✳✳ Intermediate

MEASUREMENTS

56–61 cm (22–24 in) chest; length from back neck approximately 32 cm (12½ in); sleeve seam approximately 20 cm (8 in); side seam 18 cm (7 in)

MATERIALS

- Sirdar Sublime Cashmerino:
- 5 x 50 g ball pebble, shade 006
- Knitting needles size 3.75 mm (UK 9 / US 5) and 4 mm (UK 8 / US 6)
- 6 matching buttons

TENSION

22 sts x 28 rows st st = 10 cm (4 in) square when knitted using 4 mm (Uk 8 / US 6) knitting needles

SPECIAL ABBREVIATIONS

Tw2f = Knit into front of second st on needle, do not slip st off needle, knit the first st in the usual way and slip both sts off needles together.

Tw2b = Knit into back of second st on needle, do not slip st off needle, knit the first st in the usual way and slip both sts off needles together.

BACK

Using 3.75 mm (UK 9 / US 5) knitting needles and yarn, cast on 68 sts
Work in k1, p1 rib for 8 rows.
Change to 4 mm (UK 8 / US 6) knitting needles and work in st st for 44 rows.
(Adjust length here if required.)

Shape Armholes

Cast off 6 sts at beg of next 2 rows (56 sts).
Work in pattern for yoke.
Row 1: P3, tw2f, *p4, tw2f* rep from * to * to last 3 sts, p3.
Row 2: K3, *p2, k4* to last 3 sts, p3.
Row 3: P3, tw2b, *p4, tw2b* rep from * to * to last 3 sts, p3.
Row 4: As row 2.
These 4 rows form pattern Work 36 more rows in pattern.

Shape Shoulders

Keeping pattern correct, cast off 8 sts at beg of next 4 rows.
Cast off.

LEFT FRONT

Using 3.75 mm (UK 9 / US 5) knitting needles, cast on 32 sts.
Work in k1, p1 rib for 8 rows.
Change to 4 mm (UK 8 / US 6) knitting needles and work in st st for 44 rows.
(Adjust length here if required.)

Shape Armhole

(RS) Cast off 6 sts, knit to end (26 sts).
Next row: Purl.

Work in Pattern for Yoke:

Row 1: P3, tw2f, *p4, tw2f* rep from * to * to last 3 sts, p3.
Row 2: K3, *p2, k4* rep from * to * to last 5 sts, p2, k3.
Row 3: P3, tw2b, *p4, tw2b* rep from * to * to last 3 sts, p3.
Row 4: As row 2.
Work another 21 rows.

Shape Neck

Keeping pattern correct, cast off 4 sts at beg of next row.
Dec 1 st at neck edge on next 3 rows, then on following 3 alt rows.
Work 5 rows.

Shape Shoulder

Cast off 8 sts at beg of next row.
Work 1 row. Cast off remaining 8 sts.

RIGHT FRONT

Using 3.75 mm (UK 9 / US 5) knitting needles, cast on 32 sts.

Work in k1, p1 rib for 8 rows.

Change to 4 mm (UK 8 / US 6) knitting needles and work in st st for 45 rows. (Adjust length here if required.)

Shape Armhole

(WS) Cast off 6 sts, purl to end (26 sts).

Work in Pattern for Yoke:

Row 1: P3, tw2f, *p4, tw2f* rep from * to * to last 3 sts, p3.

Row 2: K3, *p2, k4* rep from * to * to last 5 sts, p2, k3.

Row 3: P3, tw2b, *p4, tw2b* rep from * to * to last 3 sts, p3.

Row 4: As row 2

Work another 22 rows.

Shape Neck

Keeping pattern correct, cast off 4 sts at beg of next row.

Dec 1 st at neck edge on next 3 rows, then on following 3 alt rows.

Work 5 rows.

Shape Shoulder

Cast off 8 sts at beg of next row.

Work 1 row. Cast off remaining 8 sts.

SLEEVES

Using 3.75 mm (UK 9 / US 5) knitting needles, cast on 36 sts.

Work 10 rows k1, p1 rib.

Change to 4 mm (UK 8 / US 6) needles and work 4 rows st st.

Inc 1 st at each end of next and then every following 4th row until there are 58 sts.

Work 5 rows st st. Cast off loosely. Make 2.

NECK BAND

Join shoulder seams neatly, matching patterns.

With RS facing and using 3.75 mm (UK 9 / US 5) knitting needles, begin at left front neck edge and pick up 20 sts along left neck side, 24 sts across back neck and 20 sts down right front (64 sts).

Work 6 rows in k1, p1 rib. Cast off neatly in rib.

BUTTONHOLE BAND

With RS facing and using 3.75 mm (UK 9 / US 5) needles, and beginning at base of right front for girls or left front for boys, pick up and knit 83 sts evenly all along the front edge. Work in k1, p1 rib for 3 rows.

Buttonhole row: Rib 4, *yfwd, work 2tog, rib 13*, rep from * to * 4 more times, yfwd, work 2tog, rib 2.

Work 3 more rows in rib.

Cast off firmly in rib.

BUTTON BAND

With RS facing and using 3.75 mm (UK 9 / US 5) needles, and beginning at top of neck band on left front for girls or left front for boys, pick up and knit 83 sts evenly all along the front edge. Work in k1, p1 rib for 7 rows, cast off in rib.

To Make Up

Work in all ends neatly. Fold sleeves in half lengthways, mark centre of sleeve top and match to centre of shoulders, pin and sew sleeves in place.

Sew on buttons to correspond with buttonholes.

Striped Beach Sweater

Using cotton yarn and nautical colours make this oversized sweater for your toddler to wear on the beach as a cover up, or team it with jeans for a jaunty summer look. A neat pocket embellished with an anchor motif completes the look.

❋❋ **Intermediate**

MEASUREMENTS

To fit chest 56–61 cm (22–24 in);
sleeve seam 22 cm (8 ½in);.
length from back neck 36 cm (14 in)
Note Sleeve and side seams are adustable

TENSION

22 sts x 30 rows st st= 10 cm (4 in) square
using 4 mm (UK 8 / US 6) knitting needles

MATERIALS

◆ Rowan Pima cotton DK
◆ 5 x 50 g balls skipper, shade 062
◆ 3 x 50 g balls pampas, shade 050
◆ 2 small buttons to match skipper yarn.
◆ Knitting needles size 3.75 and 4 mm
   (UK 8 and 9 / US 5 and 6)
◆ 2 x stitch holders

BACK

Using 3.75 mm (UK 9 / US 5) knitting
needles and pampas, cast on 70 sts.
Work 8 rows in garter stitch.
Change to 4 mm (UK 8 / US 6) knitting
needles and work in st st stripes of 6 rows
skipper and 2 rows pampas until work
measures 35 cm (14 in), ending on a
purl row.

Shape Shoulders

Cast off 11 sts at beg of next 2 rows and
10 sts at beg of following 2 rows.
Leave rem 28 sts on a stitch holder.

FRONT

Work as for back until piece measures
30 cm (12 in).
Keeping continuity of the striped
sequence **Shape Neck**:
Next row: K28, turn and work on these sts
only, dec 1 st at neck edge on next
7 rows (21 sts).
Continue straight until front matches
back to shoulder ending at side edge.
Cast off 11 sts at beg of next row.
Work 1 row and cast off.

With RS facing, slip centre 14 sts onto
stitch holder. Rejoin yarn and knit to end.
Complete to match first side.

SLEEVES

Using 3.75 mm (UK 9 / US 5) knitting
needles and pampas, cast on 42 sts.
Work in garter stitch for 6 rows.
Change to 4 mm (UK 8 / US 6) knitting
needles and st st and work in stripes as
for back and front, but inc 1 st at each
end of 5th and every following 6th row
until 60 sts.
Continue straight until sleeve measures
22 cm. Cast off loosely.
Make 2.

NECKBAND

Join right shoulder seam.
Using 3.75 mm (UK 9 / US 5) knitting
needles and pampas, pick up and knit
15 st down left front neck, knit across
centre front sts from stitch holder, then
15 sts up right side of neck, finally work
across back neck sts from stitch holer
(72 sts).

Work 8 rows in garter stitch, cast off firmly.
Join left shoulder seam for 5 cm.

BUTTONHOLE BAND

Using 3.75 mm (UK 9 / US 5) knitting needles and pampas and with rs of front facing, starting at shoulder edge, pick up and knit 13 sts along the rest of the shoulder seam.
Next row: Knit.
Next row: K3, yrn twice, k2tog, k3, yrn twice, k2tog, k3.
Next row: Knit, knitting into yrn of previous row.
Next row: Knit. Cast off.

BUTTON BAND

Work as buttonhole band, omitting the yrn twice on buttonholes row and starting at the neck edge of the back.

POCKET

Using 4 mm (UK 8 / US 6) knitting needles and pampas, cast on 24 sts.
Knit 6 rows in garter stitch.

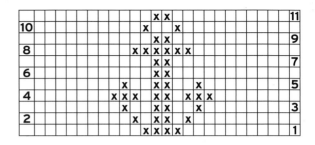

								x	x										11
10							x					x							
								x	x										9
8						x	x	x	x	x	x								
								x	x										7
6								x	x										
					x			x	x				x						5
4				x	x	x		x	x		x	x	x						
					x			x	x				x						3
2						x		x	x		x								
						x	x	x	x										1

Next row: Knit.
Next row: K2, p20, k2.
Repeat last 2 rows twice more.
Using stranding technique begin anchor motif from chart using a small ball of skipper and at the same time working 2 edge sts as before in garter stitch.

Row 1: K10 pampas, k4 skipper, k10 pampas.
Continue from chart until all 11 rows are
complete. Break yarn.
Next row: K2, p20, k2.
Work another 4 rows in st st with garter
stitch edging.
Work 6 rows garter stitch.
Cast off firmly.

To Make Up

Sew in any loose ends. Fold sleeves in half
lengthways and mark the centre top of
the sleeve. Match the marked point to the
centre of the shoulder seam. Pin and sew
in place. Join side and underarm seams on
each side.
Sew buttons on to correspond with
buttonholes.
Pin and sew the pocket in place on one side
of the sweater front.

Moccasin Slipper Socks

Just two balls of deliciously soft chunky yarn is all it takes to make these cosy slipper socks. They are sure to keep tiny toes toasty warm and snug. The two-row pattern is not too difficult to follow and gives a chunky appearance to the finished fabric. A separate sole is knitted and sewn on to provide added depth to the underside of the slipper.

❋❋ Intermediate

To fit 3–5 years

MEASUREMENTS

Length of sole 13 cm (5 in); height from sole to top 15 cm (6 in)

MATERIALS

- Wendy Norse Chunky Yarn
- 1 x 50 g ball cream shade 2700
- 1 x 50 g ball in turquoise shade 2706
- Knitting needles size 5 mm (UK 6 / US 8)

TENSION

16 sts x 24 rows st st = 10 cm (4 in) square when knitted usng 5 mm (UK 5 / US 8) knitting needles

Note For safety reasons these slippers are for indoor use on carpets only. If you wish you could purchase some Jiffy Grip fabric and sew it to the sole of the slipper to make the moccasin suitable for use on uncarpeted floors. Jiffy Grip fabric is available via the internet.

Tip The yarn is very soft and splits easily. When sewing up use short lengths of yarn and don't pull too tightly.

SPECIAL ABBREVIATIONS

KB1 = K1 below; knit into the next stitch on the row below the stitch on the needle.

Using 5 mm (UK 6 / US 8) knitting needles and cream, cast on 29 sts.
Work 5 rows garter stitch
Row 6: Knit using cream.
Row 7: *K1, kB1* repeat from * to * to end of row.
Row 8: Knit using turquoise.
Row 9: K2, *kB1, k1* rep from * to * to last.
Rows 6–9 form the pattern and are repeated. Continue in pattern, alternating colour every 2 rows for another 26 rows.

Divide for Foot

Keeping continuity of the pattern:
Next row: Pattern 19, turn.
Next row: Pattern 9, turn.
Continue in pattern on these centre 9 sts for another 16 rows.
Break yarn.
Rejoin yarn to sts on right-hand needle.
Pick up and k8 sts up right side of foot, pattern across sts of toe, pick up and k8 sts down left side of foot, then work across remaining 10 sts on left-hand needle (45 sts).
Next row: Knit.
Work 10 rows in garter stitch using cream.

Decrease for Foot

Next row: K1, k2tog, k14, k2tog, k7, k2tog, k14, k2tog, k1 (41 sts)
Next row: Knit.
Next row: K1, k2tog, k12, k2tog, k7, k2tog, k12, k2tog, k1 (37 sts).
Next row: Knit.
Next row: K1, k2tog, k10, k2tog, k7, k2tog, k10, k2tog, k1 (33 sts).
Next row: Knit.
Next row: K1, k2tog, k8, k2tog, k7, k2tog, k8, k2tog, k1 (29 sts).
Cast off.

SOLE

Work in garter stitch. Make 2.
Using turquoise and size 5 mm (UK 6/ US 8) needles cast on 6 sts.
Knit 1 row.
Inc 1 st at each end of next and foll alt

rows until you have 12 sts.

Work 8 rows.

Dec 1 stitch at each end of next row.

Work 6 rows.

Inc 1 stitch at each end of next row.

Work 12 rows.

Dec 1 stitch at each end of next and foll
alt rows until 6 sts remain. Cast off. (This
is the toe end.)

To Make Up

Sew in ends. Join leg and foot seam.
Pin sole in place, matching toe to toe of
slipper and making sure that the rows on
each side of the foot are even. Sew neatly
in place all around.

Take lengths of both yarn colours and
wind them into a tassel. Wind yarn
around the top firmly and secure with
a few stitches. Make another tassel to
match. Sew to the sides of the slippers.

Scandinavian Sweater and Hat

This beautiful set is not for the feint hearted! The patterning, although not complicated, requires plenty of concentration when following charts and shaping neck and sleeves. I have stranded the yarn not in use across the back of the work but unless you are experienced at doing this then weaving the yarn in on every third or fourth stitch might prove easier.

❋❋ Intermediate

SWEATER MEASUREMENTS

Chest 56–61 / 61–66 cm (22 x 24 / 24–26 in);
length from back neck (adjustable)
34 / 40 cm (13 / 16 in)
sleeve: (adjustable) 29 / 34 cm (11 / 13 In)

SWEATER MATERIALS

- Rico Essentials Merino DK
- 7 x 50 g balls in jeans (blue), shade 27 (A)
- 2 x 50 g balls in ecru, shade 60 (B)
- Knitting needles, size 3.75 and 4.5 mm (UK 9 / US 5)
- Stitch holder

HAT MEASUREMENTS

Circumference 41–46 cm (16–18 in) when slightly stretched

TENSION

22 sts and 28 rows st st = 10 cm (4 in) square using 4.5 mm (UK 7 / US 7) knitting needles

measures 29 (34) cm /11 (13) in) ending on a purl row. Cast off.

NECKBAND

Join right shoulder seam. Using 3.75 mm (UK 9 / US 5) knitting needles and main colour, pick up and knit 13 (17) sts down side of neck, 27 sts from front neck, 13 (17) sts from other side of neck and 27 (29) sts from back neck.
Work 9 rows k2, p2 rib.
Join in contrast colour and work 4 rows k2, p2 rib.
Rejoin main colour and work another 8 rows k2, p2 rib. Cast off loosely.

To Make Up

Work in all ends neatly. Lightly press all pieces using a warm iron and a damp cloth. Join left shoulder seam. Fold neckband in half to wrong side, catch down making sure you maintain the elasticity of the ribbing.
Fold sleeve in half lengthways, mark the centre of the top sleeve and match it to shoulder seam. Pin and sew in place neatly with back stitch. Repeat for other sleeve. Sew side and sleeve seams, matching patterning.

HAT

Using 3.75 mm (UK 9 / US 5) knitting needles and contrast colour, cast on 110 sts.
Work 2 rows, k2, p2 rib. Change to main colour and work in k2, p2 rib for another 8 cms (3 in). Dec 1 st on last row (109 sts). Change to 4.5 mm (UK 7 / US 7) knitting needles and contrast colour, work 2 rows st st.

Edge Pattern
Row 1: *K1A, k5B*, repeat to last st, k1A.
Row 2: *P2A, *p3B, p3A* repeat to last 2 sts, p2A.
Row 3: K3A, *k1B, k5A* repeat to last 4 sts, k1B, k3A.
Work 3 rows st st in main colour.
Work from chart B. Continue in snowflake pattern until work measures 10 (12) cm (4-4½ in) from start of st st ending on a purl row. Continue in main colour only.

Crown Shaping

Row 1: K1, (k2tog, k4) to end.

Row 2: Purl.

Row 3: K1. (k2tog, k3) to end.

Row 4: Purl.

Row 5: K1, (k2tog, k2) to end.

Row 6: Purl.

Row 7: K2, (k2tog, k1) to end.

Row 8: Purl.

Row 9: K1, (k2tog) to end.

Row 10: Purl.

Repeat rows 9 and 10 once.

Break off yarn and run through remaining stitches on needle, draw up tight and fasten off.

To Make Up

Sew side seam matching pattern as you do. Reverse seam on turn back. Make a large pompon using both colours. Sew securely to centre of crown.

Finnley the Fish

Who can resist this cute and fabulous toy fish? With his bright colours
and multi textures he will delight any young child. Made using pure wool and
simple knitting stitches he can be knitted in just a couple of evenings.
Use any DK yarns from your stash. Sew him up very firmly.
especially when attaching the eyes and fins.

✳✳ **Intermediate**

MEASUREMENTS

32 cm (13 in) from tip of nose to tail.

MATERIALS

- Patons Fairytale Colour 4 me DK in the
  following colours:
- 1 x 50 g ball blue, shade 4954
- 1 x 50 g yellow, shade 4960
- 1 x 50 g random stripe, shade 4970
- 1 x 50 g orange, shade 4951
- 1 x 50 g lime green, shade 4952
- Oddments of white, shade 4973 and black
  shade 4969, for eyes
- Knitting needles size 4 mm (UK 8 / US 6)
- Crochet hook size 4 mm (UK 8 / US G/8)
- Fiberfil toy stuffing
- 2 x small circles of black and 2 small circles
  of white felt

SPECIAL ABBREVIATION

MB = Make Bobble. K4 times into next st,
knitting alternately into the back and the front
of the stitch, turn, knit 4, turn, p4, slip second,
third, fourth stitch over first stitch.
SKPSO = Slip 1, knit 1, pass slipped stitch over

Lace and Cable Hat and Mittens

Pretty shaded yarn and a sweet lace and cable stitch are combined to make this chunky warm hat for little girls. A fluffy pompom adds a finishing touch. Team with mittens to make a super cute set for winter outings.

❋❋ **Intermediate (hat) * Beginner (mittens)**

MEASUREMENTS

To fit 3 (5) years (hat). The pattern is quite stretchy.
Mittens fit size 3–5 years

MATERIALS

• James Brett Baby Marble yarn
• 1 x 100 g ball in shade BM11
• Knitting needles size 5 mm (UK 6 / US 8)

TENSION

19 sts x 24 rows st st = 10 cm (4 in) square

SPECIAL ABBREVIATIONS

C6B = Cable 6 sts to the back: Slip first 3 sts onto a cable needle, leave at back of work, knit next 3 sts, then knit the 3 sts from the cable needle.

M1 = Make 1 stitch by picking up the strand that lies between the stitch you are working and the next stitch on the needle, and knitting into the back of it.

Skpso = Slip 1, knit 1, pass slipped stitch over.

Tip There is sufficient yarn to make the girls' hat and mittens, or two pairs of mittens.

Using 5 mm (UK 6 / US 8) knitting
needles and yarn, cast on 94 sts.
Work in k2, p2 rib for 16 rows, dec 1 st on
last row (93 sts).

Begin Pattern

Next row: (RS) *P3, k2tog, yfwd, k2, yfwd,
skpso* rep from * to * to last 3 sts, p3.

Next row: *K3, p6*, rep from * to * last
3 sts, k3.

Repeat the last 2 rows three more times.

Next row: *P3, c6B* rep from * to * to last
6 sts, p3.

Next row: *K3, p6*, rep from * to * last
3 sts, k3.

The last 10 rows form the pattern. Repeat
them twice more, ending on a ws row.

Decrease for Crown

Row 1: *P1, p2tog, k6*, to last 3 sts, p2tog,
p1.

Row 2 and following even rows: Knit all
knit sts and purl all purl sts.

Row 3: P2, *k2, k2tog, k2, p2tog * rep to
last 2 sts, p2.

Row 5: P2, *K2tog, k1, k2tog, p1*, rep to
last 2 sts, p2.

Row 7: P2, *sl1, k2tog, psso, p1* to last

4 sts, sl1, k2tog, psso, p2.

Row 9: P1, *k2tog*, rep across row, to last
2 sts, p2tog.

Break yarn and run through stitches on
needle, gather up and secure. Sew side
seam neatly.

Make a large pompom and sew to the top
of the hat securely.

RIGHT MITTEN

Using 5 mm (UK6 / US 8) knitting
needles, cast on 30 sts.
Work in k2, p2 rib for 18 rows.
Work 2 rows st st **

Shape Thumb

Next row: K16, m1, k1, m1, k13.

Next and following alt rows: Purl.

Next row: K16, m1, k3, m1, k13.

Next row: K16, m1, k5, m1, k13

Next row: K16, m1, k7, m1, k13.

Next row: Purl (38 sts).

Work Thumb

Next row: K25, turn, cast on 1 st.

Next row: P10, turn, cast on 1 st.

***Work 6 rows in st st on these 11sts.

Next row: K2tog across row to last st, k1.

Break yarn and thread through sts, draw up and fasten off. Sew the thumb seam. With rs facing, rejoin yarn. Pick up and knit 2 sts from the base of the thumb, knit to end of row (31 sts).

Next row: Purl.

Work 10 rows st st ending in purl.

Shape Top

Row 1: K1, k2tog, k10, k2tog, k1, k2tog, k10, k2tog, k1 (27 sts).

Row 2: Purl.

Row 3: K1, k2tog, k8, k2tog, k1, k2tog, k8, k2tog, k1 (23 sts).

Row 4: Purl.

Row 5: K1, k2tog, k6, k2tog, k1, k2tog, k6, k2tog, k1 (19 sts).

Row 6: Purl.

Row 7: K1, k2tog, k4, k2tog, k1, k2tog, k4, k2tog, k1 (15 sts).

Row 8: Purl. Cast off.

LEFT MITTEN

Work as for Right Mitten to **

Shape Thumb

Row 1: K13, m1, k1, m1, k16.

Row 2 and following even rows: Purl.

Row 3: K13, m1, k3, m1, k16.

Row 5: K13, m1, k5, m1, k16.

Row 7: K13, m1, k7, m1, k16.

Row 8: Purl.

Work Thumb

Next row: K22, turn.

Next row: P9, turn.

Complete as for Right Mitten from ***

To Make Up

The purl side is the right side of the mitten. Sew side seam and top of mitten. Fold back cuffs.

Make two small pompoms and attach firmly to the side seams on both mittens, catching the cuffs in place with a few stitches as you work.

Cable Tank Top

Unusual stitch patterning, along with a lovely soft bamboo yarn give this neat tank top a modern look. Make the little man in your life look extra smart for special outings when you team the top with a shirt or go for a casual look with a long sleeved T-shirt and jeans. Take care to keep the continuity of patterning correct when shaping the armholes and neck.

✳✳✳ **Experienced**

MEASUREMENTS

Chest 56–61 cm (22–24 in);
length from back neck 30 cm (12 in)

MATERIALS

- Sirdar Snuggly Baby Bamboo
- 5 x 50 g balls groovy green, shade 122
- Knitting needles size 3.75 and 4 mm
  (UK 8 and 9 / US 5 and 6)
- 2 stitch holders
- Safety pin

TENSION

22 sts x 28 rows st st = 10 cm (4in) square using 4 mm (UK 8 / US 6) knitting needles

Tip Mark down the rows as you work them when decreasing for the V-neck shaping, so that you won't forget which row you are on if you leave your work.

Plaited Hairband

Make your fashion-conscious little girl a trendy headband using a luxurious kid mohair and lambswool mix. Complete the look with a pretty knitted bow, finished off with a cute butterfly button. You could knit this project in a weekend.

❋ **Easy**

MEASUREMENTS
To fit 2–4 years old

MATERIALS
- Rowan Kid Classic
- 1 x 50 g ball feather, shade 828
- 1 x 50 g ball tea rose, shade 854
- 1 x 50 g ball drought, shade 876
- Butterfly button
- Knitting needles size 4.5 mm (UK 7 / US 6)

The head band is made in three strips, which are plaited together.

Using feather and 4.5 mm (UK 7 / US 6) knittingneedles, cast on 14 sts.
Work in st st, beginning with a knit row, and continue until strip measures 53 cm (21 in). Cast off.
Make 1 strip using tea rose and 1 strip using drought.

BOW

Using tea rose and 4.5 mm (UK 7 / US 6) knitting needles, cast on 8 sts.
Work in garter stitch for 20 cm (8 in). Cast off.

To Make Up

Secure the ends of the strips together
with some matching yarn. Plait the strips
neatly and evenly. Secure the ends.
To join the band into a circle loosen each
end of the strips then weave them inside
each other to give the plait continuity.
Tuck in the ends and sew in place.
To make the bow, join the two short ends
of the strip together. Fold in half with the
join at the centre back. With a needle
and matching yarn, thread the yarn
through the centre of the bow from top to
bottom, draw up to gather the strip and
accentuate the bow. Sew firmly in place.
Sew the bow to the headband to cover
the join. Stitch the butterfly button to the
centre of the bow.

Puff-sleeve Angora Cardigan

This adorable cardigan is made in sumptuous angora and lamb's wool and weighs very little. The colours available are just stunning so you can chose subtle shades or pick more vibrant tones. A pretty fairisle flower pattern decorates the lower part of the cardigan, which is worked in one piece up to the armholes.

❋❋❋ **Experienced**

MEASUREMENTS

Chest 56–61 cm (22–24 in);
length from underarm 20cm (8 in)
sleeve seam 5 cm (2 in);
length from back neck 30cm (12 in)

MATERIALS

- ◆ Orkney Angora 50/50 DK
- ◆ info@orkneyangora.co.uk
- ◆ 2 x 50 g balls beige
- ◆ 1 x 50 g ball blackberry
- ◆ 1 x 50 g ball heather
- ◆ Knitting needles size 3.25 and 4 mm (UK 10 and 8 / US 4 and 6)

- • 2 stitch holders
- • 5 flower buttons

TENSION

24 sts x 26 rows st st = 10 cm square worked on 4 mm (UK 8 / US 6) needles

The back and fronts are knitted in one piece to the armholes.

Using 3.75 mm (UK 9 / US 5) knitting needles and blackberry, cast on 144 sts
Work 2 rows k1, p1 rib.
Change to beige and work 8 rows k1, p1 rib.
Change to 4 mm (UK 8 / US 6) knitting needles and work 4 rows st st in beige beginning with a knit row. Joining in colours as indicated from chart, work as follows:
Next row: K3 beige, *work 6-stitch repeat from chart* between dotted lines, to last 3 sts, k3 beige.
Work next 5 rows from chart.
Work 6 rows st st in beige.
Next row: K6 beige, *work 6-stitch repeat from chart* to last 6 sts, k6 beige.
Work next 5 rows from chart.
Work 6 rows st st in beige.
Next row: K3 beige, *work 6-stitch repeat from chart* to last 3 sts, k3 beige.
Work next 5 rows from chart.
Work 6 rows st st in beige.
Next 2 rows: Using heather, work in garter st.
Next 2 rows: Using blackberry, work in garter st.
Next 2 rows: Using beige, work 2 rows st st.
Break blackberry and heather and continue in beige only.

Divide for Back and Fronts
Next row: K33, cast off 6 sts, k66, cast off 6 sts, k33.
Next row: P33, slip these sts onto a stitch holder for left front. Rejoin yarn. Purl 66 sts for back. Leave remaining 33 sts on another stitch holder for right front.

BACK
Dec 1 st at each end of the next 3 rows.
Dec 1 st at each end of the next and following alt rows until there are 54 sts.
Continue on these sts in st st until work measures 13 cm (5 in) ending with a purl row.

Shape Shoulders
With the rs facing, cast off 6 sts, k10 (including the st already on the needle after cast off), turn and cast off 3 sts, purl

to end.

Cast off remaining sts.

LEFT FRONT

Return sts for left front to needle.

Dec 1 st at armhole edge on next 3 rows,
then on the following 3 alt rows (27 sts).

Work straight until 19 rows less than back
to shoulder shaping ending on a rs row.

Shape Neck

Cast off 6 sts at beg of next row.

Dec 1 st at neck edge on next 3 rows.

Dec 1 st on next and following 3 alt rows,
then on following 4th row at neck edge.

Work 3 rows ending on a ws row.

Shape Shoulders

Cast off 5 sts at beg of next row.

Purl 1 row. Cast off.

RIGHT FRONT

Return remaining stitches on holder
to needle.

Dec 1 st at armhole edge on next 3 rows,
then on the following 3 alt rows (27 sts).

Work straight until 18 rows less than back
to shoulder shaping ending on a ws row.

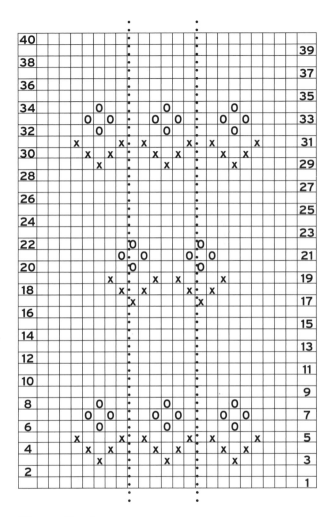

Shape Neck

Cast off 6 sts at beg of next row.

Dec 1 st at neck edge on next 3 rows.

Dec 1 st on next and following 3 alt rows,

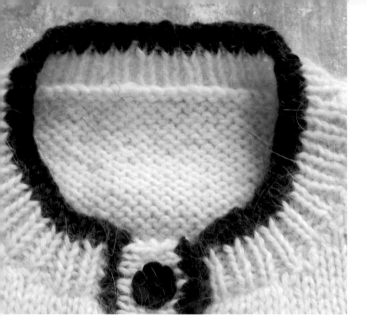

then on following 4th row at neck edge.

Work 3 rows ending on a rs row.

Shape Shoulders

Cast off 5 sts at beg of next row.

Purl 1 row and cast off.

SLEEVES

Using 3.25 mm (UK 10 / US 4) knitting needles and blackberry, cast on 63 sts.

Row 1: *K1, p1* rep from * to * to last st, k1.

Row 2: *P1, k1* rep from * to * to last st, p1.

Change to beige.

Work 2 rows rib as above.

Change to 4 mm (UK 8 / US 6)

knitting needles.

Inc row: K17, inc in each of next 28 sts, k17 (90 sts).

Work 7 rows st st

Shape Top

Cast off 3 sts at beg of next 2 rows.

Dec 1 st at each end of next 5 rows, then on the following 3 alt rows.

Dec 1 st at each end of every row until 42 sts remain, ending on a knit row.

Next row: P3tog across row.

Cast off firmly.

Join shoulder seams neatly.

Make 2.

NECKBAND

Using 3.25 mm (UK 10 / US 4) knitting needles and beige, and beginning at right the front edge, pick up and knit 19 sts up right front neck, 30 sts from back neck and 19 sts down left front neck (68 sts).

Work in k1, p1 rib for 6 rows.

Change to blackberry and work 2 rows of k1, p1 rib. Cast off neatly in rib.

BUTTON BAND

Using 3.25 mm (UK 10 / US 4) knitting
needles and blackberry, begin at top of
left front band and pick up and knit 79 sts
evenly down entire front.
Work 1 row in k1, p1 rib.
Change to beige and work 6 rows in
k1, p1 rib.
Change to blackberry and work 1 row
k1, p1 rib. Cast off in rib.

BUTTONHOLE BAND

Using 3.25 mm (UK 10 / US 4) knitting
needles and blackberry, begin at base of
right front, pick up and knit 79 sts evenly
along entire front and neck band..
Work 1 row k1, p1 rib.
Change to beige and work 2 rows in
k1, p1 rib.
Buttonhole row: K4, cast off 2 sts, *k15
(counting the st left on needles after
casting off) cast off 2 sts*, repeat from
* to * 3 more times, k4.
Next row: Work in rib, cast on 2 sts over
each of the buttonholes made in previous
row.

Work 2 more rows k1, p1 rib in beige.
Change to blackberry and work 1 row in
rib as set.
Cast off in rib.

To Make Up

Sew in any loose ends of yarns.
Join seams.
Pin sleeve in place around armhole,
easing fullness to fit evenly around the
top section. Sew in place. Repeat with the
other sleeve.
Sew buttons on to correspond with
buttonholes.

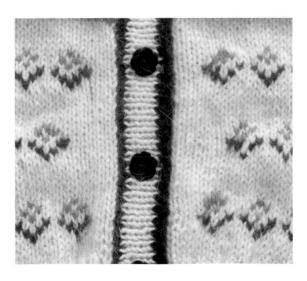

Puff-sleeve Angora Cardigan

Boys Cable Hat and Mittens

Knit this chunky cable hat for the little man in your life. It will keep him snug and warm while he plays outside during the colder weather. The pattern stitch is quite simple to follow and by knitting into the back of the stitches it gives extra definition to the cable detail. Team the hat with some matching mittens.

✹✹ Intermediate

MEASUREMENTS

To fit 3–5 years. The pattern is quite stretchy.

MATERIALS

- James Brett Marble yarn
- 1 x 100g ball shade MT17
- Knitting needle size 5 mm (UK 6 / US 8)
- Cable needle

TENSION

19 sts x 24 rows st st= 10 cm (4 in) square using knitting needles

SPECIAL ABBREVIATIONS

KB1 = Knit into the back of the stitch.

C6Bk = Slip first 3 sts onto a cable needle, leave at back of work, KB1, p1, KB1 over next 3 sts, now KB1, p1, KB1 over the 3 sts from the cable needle.

Note There will be sufficient yarn to make both the boys hat and mittens, or two pairs of mittens.

k4*.

Row 5: K13, m1, k5, m1, *k4, p1, KB1, p1, [KB1 twice], p1, KB1, p1, k4.

Row 7: K13, m1, k7, m1, *k4, p1, kB1, p1, [KB1 twice], p1, KB1, p1, k4.

Row 8: As row 2.

Work Thumb

Next row: K22, turn.

Next row: P9, turn.

Complete as Right Mitten from ***

To Make Up

Sew side seam and top of mitten. Fold back cuffs.

LEFT MITTEN

Work as for Right Mitten to **

Shape Thumb

Row 1: K13, m1, k1, m1, *k4, p1, KB1, p1, [KB1 twice], p1, kB1, p1, k4*.

Row 2 and all even rows: Knit all knit sts and purl all purl sts.

Row 3: K13, m1, k3, m1, *k4, p1, CB6k, p1,

Overdress

A sculptured pattern gives this little overdress a special look. Team it with tights for a pretty look or wear it over jeans for a more casual outfit. Knitted in a beautiful soft yarn, which is available in a range of delicious colours, you will find it hard to decide which one to use.

❋❋❋ Experienced

To fit 2–4 years

MEASUREMENTS

Chest 71 cm (31 in) around chest; length from back neck 48 cm (19 in), adjustable; sleeve seam with cuff turned back 6 cm (2½ in)

MATERIALS

- 7 x 50g balls Sirdar Sublime Baby Cashmere/Merino/Silk DK in ragdoll, shade 0244
- Knitting needles size 3.25 and 4 mm (UK 8 and 10 / US 4 and 6)
- 2 stitch holders
- 4 flower buttons

TENSION

22st x 28 rows st st = 10 cm (4 in) square using 4 mm (Uk 8 / US 6)

SLEEVES

With 3.25 mm (UK 10 / US 4) knitting needles and main yarn, cast on 55 sts, work 10 cm (4 in) garter stitch.

Change to 4 mm (UK 8 / US 6) knitting needles. Beginning with a knit row, work in st st until piece measures 15 cm (6 in) ending on a purl row.

Shape Armholes

Cast off 5 sts at the beginning of the next 2 rows.

Work 2 rows straight in st st.

Next row: K2, k2tog, work to last 4 sts, k1, sl1, psso, k2.

Work 3 rows st st.

Next row: K2, k2tog, work to last 4 sts, k1, sl1, psso, k2.

Next row: Purl.

Continue shaping as rows 5 and 6 until 9 sts remain. Leave sts on a holder.

Work second sleeve to match.

BACK

Using 4 mm (UK 8 / US 6) knitting needles, cast on 99 sts fairly loosely.

Row 1: K1, yrn, p5, p3tog, *p5, yrn, k1, yrn, p5, p3tog*, rep from * to * to last 6 sts, p5, yfwd, k1.

Row 2 and all even rows: Purl.

Rows 3, 5, 7, 9 and 11: Work as row 1.

Row 13: K1, yfwd, sl1, k1, psso, yrn, p3, p3tog, *p3, yfwd, k2tog, yfwd, k1, yfwd, sl1, k1, psso, yrn, p3, p3tog* rep from * to * to last 6 sts, p3, yfwd, k2tog, yfwd, k1.

Row 15: K1, yfwd, k1, sl1, k1, psso, yrn, p2, p3tog, *p2, yfwd, k2tog, k1, yfwd, k1, yfwd, sl1, k1, psso, yrn, p2, p3tog* rep from * to * to last 6 sts, p2, yfwd, k2tog, k1, yfwd, k1.

Row 17: K1, yfwd, k2, sl1, k1, psso, yrn, p1, p3tog, *p1, yfwd, k2tog, k2, yfwd, k1, yfwd, k2, sl1, k1, psso, yrn, p1, p3tog* rep from * to * to last 6 sts, p1, yfwd, k2tog, k2, yfwd, k1.

Row 19: K1, yfwd, k3, sl1, k1, psso, yrn, p3tog, *yfwd, k2tog, k3, yfwd, k1, yfwd, k3, sl1, k1, psso, yrn, p3tog* rep from * to * to last 6 sts, yfwd, k2tog, k3, yfwd, k1.

Row 21: K4, k2tog, yfwd, k2 *k1, yfwd, sl1, k1, psso, k7, k2tog, yfwd, k2*, rep from * to * to last 7 sts, k1, yfwd, k2tog, k4.

Row 23: K3, k2tog, yfwd, k3, *k2, yfwd, sl1, k1, psso, k5, k2tog, yfwd, k3* rep from

* to * to last 7 sts, k2, yfwd, sl1, k1, psso, k3.

Row: 25: K2, k2tog, yfwd, k4, *k3, yfwd, sl1, k1, psso, k3, k2tog, yfwd, k4* rep from * to * to last 7 sts, k3, yfwd, sl1, k1, psso, k2.

Row 27: K1, k2tog, yfwd, k5, *k4, yfwd, sl1, k1, psso, k1, k2tog, yfwd, k5*, rep from * to * to last 7 sts, K4, yfwd, sl1, k1, psso, k1.

Row 29: K2tog, yfwd, k6, *k5, yfwd, sl1, k2tog, psso, yfwd, k6*, rep from * to * to last 7 sts, k5, yfwd, sl1, k1, psso.

Row 30: Purl.

Continue in st st, dec 1 st at each end of the next and every following 8th row until there are 83 sts on the needleand work measures approx 30 cm (12 in). Adjust length here if required.

Shape Armholes

Cast off 5 sts at the beginning of the next two rows.

Next row: K2, k2tog, work to last 4 sts, k1, sl1, psso, k2.

Next row: Purl.

Continue as for last 2 rows until 31 sts remain. Slip sts onto a holder.

FRONT

Work as back until there are 47 sts.

Shape Neck

Next row: K2, k2tog, k12, turn and work on these sts for first side of neck.

Row 1: P2tog, purl to end.

Row 2: K2, k2tog, work to last 2 sts, k2tog.

Continue as on last 2 rows until 8 sts remain.

Continue to decrease at armhole edge only until you have 3 sts.

P3tog and fasten off.

Slip next 15 sts onto a holder for front neck.

Rejoin yarn to remaining sts and work other side of neck.

Next row: K12, skpso, k2.

Complete to match first side, reversing instructions and working skpso instead of k2tog.

Neck Band

With 3.25 mm (UK 10 / US 4) knitting
needles and rs of work facing, pick up
and knit 15 sts down left side of neck,
knit across 15 sts on holder, 14 sts up right
side of neck, 9 sts from top of sleeve,
31 sts from back neck, and 9 sts from top
of other sleeve (93 sts).

Next row: Working in garter stitch, k9,
dec 6 sts evenly across k31 sts of back of
neck, k44, (87 sts).

Continue in garter stitch for another
8 rows.

Cast off firmly in garter stitch.

Join cast off sts at left front raglan and
first 10 rows of raglan shaping.

BUTTONHOLE BAND

With rs facing and using 3.25 mm
(UK 10 / US 4) knitting needles, pick up
and knit 37 sts evenly along front raglan
edge and neckband.

Work 3 more rows garter stitch.

Buttonhole row: K2, yrn, k2tog, *k6, yrn,
k2tog*, rep from * to last st, k1.

Work 3 more rows garter stitch.

Cast off.

BUTTON BAND

With rs facing and using 3.25 mm
(UK 10 / US 4) knitting needles, pick up
and knit 37 sts evenly along back raglan
edge.

Join side and sleeve seams. Turn cuffs
back onto right side of sleeves. Sew on
buttons to correspond with button holes.

Fruit and Play Bag

Use brightly coloured yarn remnants to make these delightful smiley-faced fruit. When it's time to pack the fruit away, store them in their own carrier bag, which has been decorated with an apple tree, flowers and butterflies. Alternatively the bag is perfect for a little girl to take shopping.

✱ **Easy**

Note When making up the fruit take care to sew everything very securely if you intend to let very young children play with them.

BAG MEASUREMENTS
27 cm (10 ½ in) wide x 22 cm (9 in) tall

MATERIALS
Bag:
- Sirdar Baby Aran
- 2 x 100 g balls red poppy, shade 824
- Knitting needles size 3.75, 4 and 4.5 mm (UK 7, 8 and 9 / US 5, 6 and 7)

- Oddments of green, brown and red DK yarn for the tree
- Flower and butterfly buttons

Fruit:
- Approximately 25 g of DK yarn in: pale yellow, deep yellow, green, black, red-orange, brown and deep purple
- Knitting needles size 3.75 mm (UK 9 / US 5)
- Safety stuffing
- Black yarn for embroidery

SPECIAL ABBREVIATION
M1 = Make 1 stitch by picking up the strand of yarn that lies between the stitch you are working and the next one on the needle, and working into the back of it.

BAG

Using aran yarn and 4.5 mm (UK 7 / US 7) knitting needles, cast on 46 sts.
Work in garter stitch for 10 rows.
Row 11: Knit.
Row 12: K8, purl to last 8sts, k8.
Repeat Rows 11 and 12 another 22 times.
Work 6 rows in garter stitch.
*****Next row**: Knit.
Next row: K8, purl to last 8 sts, k8.
Repeat last 2 rows once more.
Work 4 rows in garter stitch.**
Repeat last 8 rows from * to ** 5 times more, then first 4 rows again.
Work 10 rows garter stitch. Cast off.

HANDLES

Using green dk and 4 mm (UK 8 / US 6) knitting needles, cast on 60 sts.
Knit 14 rows.
Cast off.
Make 2.

TREE

To make the trunk, using 3.75 mm (UK 9 / US 5) knitting needles and brown yarn, cast on 7 sts.
Work in k1, p1 rib for 18 rows. Cast off.
To make foliage, using 3.75 mm (UK 9 / US 5) knitting needles and green yarn, cast on 10 sts.
Next row: Inc 1 st at each end.
Next row: Knit.
Repeat last 2 rows until you have 18 sts.
Work 5 rows in st st.
Next row: Dec 1 st at each end.
Next row: Knit.
Repeat last 2 rows until 8 sts remain.
Cast off.

To Make Up

Work in all yarn ends neatly. Fold piece in half right sides together and sew side seams. Turn right side out.
Embroider red French knots to depict apples on one side of the foliage at random intervals. Pin foliage and trunk in place on the front st st panel. Sew neatly in place. Sew on flower and butterfly buttons. Pin handles in place on each side of the top of the bag. Sew firmly in place at the base.

PEAR

Using 3.75 mm (UK 9 / US 5) knitting needles and appropriate colour cast on 10 sts.

Knit 1 row.

Row 2: Increase in each stitch across row (20 sts).

Row 3: Purl.

Row 4: *K1, inc in next st* across row (30 sts).

Work 3 rows st st.

Row 8: (K2, increase in next stitch) all across row (40 sts).

Row 9: Purl.

Work 10 rows in st st.

Row 20: (K2, k2tog) across row.

Work 5 rows in st st beginning with a purl row.

Row 26: (K1, k2tog) all across row.

Work 5 rows st st beginning with a purl row.

Row 32: K2tog all across row.

Row 33: Purl.

Don't cast off, but run yarn through remaining 10 sts and pull up tightly, fasten off.

ORANGE

Using 3.75 mm (UK 9 / US 5) knitting needles and appropriate colour, cast on 10 sts.

Knit 1 row.

Row 2: Increase in each stitch across row (20 sts).

Row 3: Purl.

Row 4: *K1, inc in next st*, all across row (30 sts).

Work 3 rows st st, beginning with a purl row.

Row 8: (K2, inc in next stitch) all across row (40 sts).

Row 9: Purl.

Work 14 rows st st.

Row 24: (K2, k2tog) all across row.

Work 3 rows st st beginning with a purl row.

Row 28: (K1, k2tog) all across row.

Row 29: Purl.

Row 30: K2tog all across row.

Row 31: Purl.

Don't cast off, but run yarn through remaining 10 sts and pull up tightly, fasten off.

Row 14: K2tog across row.

Row 15: P2tog across row to last st, p1.

Row 16: K3tog, fasten off.

PLUM

Using 3.75 mm (UK 9 / US 5) knitting needles and appropriate colour, cast on 5 sts.

Row 1: Purl.

Row 2: Inc in each st to end of row (10 sts).

Row 3: Purl.

Row 4: Increase in each stitch across row (20 sts).

Row 5: Purl.

Work 4 rows st st.

Row 10: (K2, k2tog), to end.

Row 11: Purl.

Row 12: (K1, k2tog), to end.

Row 13: Purl.

APPLE

Using 3.75 mm (UK 9 / US 5) knitting needles and appropriate colour, cast on 10 sts.

Knit 1 row.

Row 2: Increase in each stitch across row (20 sts).

Row 3: Purl.

Row 4: (K1, inc in next st) all across row (30 sts).

Work 3 rows st st.

Row 8: (K2, inc in next stitch) all across row (40 sts).

Row 9: Purl.

Work 10 rows st st on these stitches.

Row 20: (K2, k2tog) all across row.

Work 3 rows st st beginning with a purl row.

Row 24: (K1, k2tog) all across row.

Row 25: Purl.

Row 26: K2tog all across row.

Row 27: Purl.

Don't cast off, but run yarn through remaining 10 sts and pull up tightly, fasten off.

LEMON

Using 3.75 mm (UK 9 / US 5) knitting needles and yellow yarn, cast on 5 sts.

Row 1: Purl.

Row 2: Inc in each st to end of row (10 sts).

Row 3: Purl.

Row 4: Inc in each stitch across row (20 sts).

Row 5: Purl.

Row 6: (K1, inc in next st), all across row (30 sts).

Row 7: Purl.

Work 4 rows st st.

Row 8: (K3, k2tog) to end.

Work 3 rows st st.

Row 12: (K2, k2tog) to end.

Row 13: Purl.

Row 14: (K1, k2tog) to end.

Row 15: Purl.

Row 16: K2tog across row.

Row 17: P2tog across row.

Row 18: K3tog, fasten off.

BANANA

Using 3.75 mm (UK 9/US 5) knitting needles and black yarn, cast on 8 sts.

Knit 2 rows garter stitch.

Break off black yarn and join in pale green.

Work 2 rows st st.

Break green yarn and join in yellow yarn.

Inc 1 st at each end of the next and every alt row until you have 14 sts.

Row 6: Purl.

Row 7: Inc in first st, k6, m1 work to last stitch, inc 1.

Work 3 rows st st beginning with a purl row.

Row 11: Inc in first st, k7, m1, k8, inc in last st (20 sts).

Work 3 rows st st beginning with a
purl row.

Row 15: Inc in first st, k9, m1, k9, inc in last
st (23 sts).

Row 16: Purl.

Row 17: Inc in first st, k10, m1, k11, inc in
last st (26 sts).

Row 18: Purl.

Row 19: Inc in first st, k12, m1, k12, inc in
last st (29 sts).

Row 20: Purl.

Work 6 rows straight in st st.

Row 27: K14, turn and purl to end.

Row 28: K15, turn and purl to end.

Row 29: K16, turn and purl to end.

Row 30: K17, turn and purl to end.

Work in st st for 6 rows ending on a
purl row.

Row 37: Dec 1 st at each end of next row.

Row 38: Purl.

Row 39: K2tog, k10, k2tog, work to last
2 sts, k2tog.

Work 3 rows st st beginning with a
purl row.

Row 43: K2tog, k9, k2tog, work to last
2 sts, k2tog.

Row 44: Purl.

Dec 1 st at each end of next and following
alternate rows until 9 sts remain.

Work 5 rows straight in st st. Cast off.

STALKS

Using 3.75 mm (UK 9 / US 5) knitting
needles and brown yarn, cast on 6 sts.
Knit 2 rows garter stitch. Cast off.

LEAVES

Using 3.75 mm (UK 9 / US 5) knitting
needles and green, cast on 5 sts.
Knit 2 rows garter stitch.

Row 3: K2, m1, k1, m1, k2 (7 sts).

Row 4: K3, p1, k3.

Row 5: K3, m1, k1, m1, k3. (9 sts).

Row 6: K4, p1, k4.

Row 7: Knit.

Repeat last 2 rows twice more.

Dec 1 st at each end of next and every following row until 3 sts remain.

Next row: K3tog, fasten off.

To Make Up the Fruit

Apple

Sew side seam of apple, stuff firmly, shape and close seam. Sew a stalk and a leaf securely to the top of the apple.

Orange

Sew and stuff as for the apple but use the reverse side of the knitting to give the textured effect of the rind. Embroider a French knot on the top and bottom of the fruit using black yarn.

Pear

Sew and stuff as for the apple, remembering that the pear will be "fatter" at the bottom and taper toward the top. Attach leaves to top of pear.

Lemon:

Sew up, stuff and shape as for the apple.

Plum

Sew up, stuff and shape as for the apple. Attach a stalk and leaf.

Banana

Sew the side seam of the banana. Stuff firmly. Bend the fruit a little in the centre to give a curved shape. Thread a needle with yellow yarn and work three rows of chain stitch along the length of the banana to give definition to the skin. Use black yarn to embroider happy faces onto the fruit.

Striped Socks

A beautifully soft cashmere-and-wool-mix yarn is used to make these little socks. Three balls of yarn are used at the same time for the shaping, which make sthe pattern a little tricky. It is simple to add length in the leg and also in the foot to create bigger sizes.

✳✳ Intermediate

To fit 3–5 years; foot and leg length is adjustable

Tip The socks can be made just using one shade of yarn if desired

TENSION
24 sts x 32 rows st st = 10 cm (4 in) square
using 3.75 mm (UK 9 / US 5) knitting needles

MATERIALS
- Rowan Cashsoft DK
- 1 x 50g ball in poppy, shade 512 (A)
- 1 x 50g ball blue jacket, shade 535 (B)
- Knitting needles size 3.75 mm (UK 9 / US 5)

Stripe pattern is knitted by alternating
2 rows A with 2 rows B st st.

Make 2.

Using size 3.75 mm (UK 9 / US 5) knitting
needles and **A,** cast on 43 sts.
Row 1: K1, p1 , rep to last st, k1.
Row 2: P1, k1, rep to last st, p1.
Work in k1, p1 rib for 2 rows.
Change to B and work another 14 rows
in rib.
Change to st st and work *2 rows B,
2 rows A*, rep from * to * twice more, then
work 2 rows B. (Adjust length of leg at this
point, if required).

Shape Heel
Using poppy, k12, turn, work in st st for
another 15 rows, ending with a purl
row, turn.
Next row: K3, k2tog, k1, turn, sl1, p4, turn.
Next row: K4, k2tog, k1, turn, sl1, p5, turn.
Next row: K5, k2tog, k1, turn, sl1, p6, turn.
Next row: K6, k2tog, k1 (8 sts).
Next row: Purl.
Using A, k8, pick up and k10 sts along side

of heel, knit to end of row.
Next row: P12, turn and work on these sts
for second side of heel.
Work 15 rows st st ending with a knit row.
Work other side of heel as follows:
Next row: P3, p2tog, p1, turn, sl1, k4, turn.
Next row: P4, p2tog, p1, turn, sl1, k5, turn.
Next row: P5, p2tog, p1, turn, sl1, k6, turn.
Next row: Knit.
Next row: P6, p2tog, p1 (8 sts).
Now pick up and purl 10 sts along side of
heel, purl to end of row.
Note To maintain the striped pattern
over the instep you will need to join in a
separate ball of A at each end of the row
and join in B as required.
Continue heel shaping as follows:
Next row: K16, k2tog, k19B, k2tog tbl, k16.
Next row: P17A, k19B, k17A.
Next row: K15, k2tog, k19A, sl1, k1,
k2tog tbl, k15.
Next row: Purl using A.
Next row: K14, k2tog, k19B, K2tog tbl, k14.
Next row: P15A, 19B, 15A.
Next row: Using A k13, k2tog, k19, K2tog
tbl, k13.

Next row: Purl using A.

Next row: K12, k2tog, k19B, k2togtbl, k12.

Next row: P13A, p19B, p13A.

Next row: Using A k11, k2tog, k19,
K2tog tbl, k11.

Next row: Using A purl across all sts
(43 sts).

Continue on these sts, working
2 rows B, 2 rows A until work measures
desired length, ending on a purl row of a
B stripe.

Shape Toe

Next row: Using A only for toe, k9, k2tog,
k2, k2tog tbl, k13, k2tog, k2, k2tog tbl, k9.

Next row: Purl.

Next row: K8, k2tog, k2, k2tog tbl, k11,
k2tog, k2, k2tog tbl, k8.

Next row: Purl.

Next row: K7, k2tog, k2, k2tog tbl, k9,
k2tog, k2, k2tog tbl, k7.

Continue decreasing 4 sts on every alt
row, until 19 sts remain ending on a purl
row. Cast off.

To Make Up

Sew in all ends neatly. Sew foot and back
seam using a flat seam. Turn cuff back on
top of sock, if required.

Shawl-neck Sweater

Wide stocking stitch stripes and a shawl collar make this a perfect rough and tumble sweater.It will keep a little person warm and snug on outings to the park or when playing in the garden. Aran-weight yarn makes the sweater quick to knit and the range of colours available are sure to suit all tastes. Omit the stripes and make it using one colour, if you like.

❋❋ **Intermediate**

To fit 1–2 years (2–3 years/3–4 years)

TENSION

18 sts x 24 rows st st = 10 cm (4 in) squyare using 4.5 mm (UK 7 / US 7) knitting needles

MEASUREMENTS

Chest 51–56 (56–61, 61–66) cm,
20–22 (22–24, 24–26) in;
length from back neck 30 (34, 40) cm ,
12 (13½, 16) in;
sleeve length 17 (20, 24) cm, 7 (8 9½) in

MATERIALS

- Sirdar Supersoft Aran
- 2 (2, 3) x 100 g balls river blue, shade 877 (A)
- 1 (1, 2) x 100 g.ball cream, shade 831 (B)
- Knitting needles size 4 and 4.5 mm (UK 7 and 8 / US 6 and 7)
- Stitch holder.

Note Carry yarn not in use loosely up side of work.

BACK

Using 4 mm (UK 8/ US 6) knitting needles and A, cast on 50 (56, 60) sts. Work in k2, p2 rib for 6 cm (2 1/2 in) for all sizes.

Change to 4.5 mm (UK 7 / US 7) knitting needles. Join in yarn B and change to st st, working in stripes of 6 rows yarn A and 6 rows yarn B. Continue until back measures 28 (32, 38) cm or 11 (12½, 15 in) ending with a purl row.

Shape Shoulders

Cast off 8 (9, 9) sts at beg of next 2 rows, and 8 (9, 10) sts at beg of following 2 rows. Cast off remaining 18 (20, 22) sts.

FRONT

Work as for back until front measures 19 (23, 27) cm or 71/2 (9, 101/2 in) ending with a purl row.

Keeping continuity of stripe pattern,

Shape Neck as follows

Next row: K16 (18, 19) turn and work on this side first, leaving remaining sts on a holder.

Continue until work measures 28 (32, 38)

cm or 11 (12½, 15 in) ending on a purl row.

Shape Shoulder

Next row: Cast off 8 (9, 9) sts, work to end.

Next row: Purl.

Next row: Cast off remaining stitches. Return to stitches on holder and rejoin appropriate colour.

Cast off 18 (20, 22) sts for centre neck, knit to end.

Complete to match first half, reversing shoulder shapings.

SLEEVES

Using thumb method, 4 mm (UK 8 / US 6) knitting needles and A, cast on 35 (35, 37) sts

Work in k2, p2 rib for 5 cm (2 in) for all sizes.

Change to 4.5 mm (UK 7 / US 7) knitting needles.

Join in B and work in stripe pattern as for back, AT THE SAME TIME inc 1 st at each end of the 5th and every following 14th (6th, 8th) row until there are 39 (45, 49) sts. Continue without shaping until sleeve measures 17 (20, 24) cm or 7 (8, 91/2) in ending on a purl row.

Shape Top of Sleeve

Cast off 3 (4, 3) sts at beg of next 2 (4, 8) rows.

Cast off 4 (5, 4) sts at beg of next 6 (4, 4) rows.

Cast off remaining stitches.

Make 2.

SHAWL COLLAR

Using 4 mm (UK 8 / US 6) knitting needles and A, cast on 116 (116, 124) sts.

Row 1: P1, k2, (p2, k2 to last st), p1.

Row 2: K1 (p2, k2 to last 3 sts), p2, k1.

Rows 1 and 2 set the rib pattern. Continue in rib until collar measures 9 (10, 12) cm or 31/2 (4, 41/2 in) ending on a row 2. Cast off loosely in rib.

Making Up

Sew in all yarn ends. Press all pieces following yarn manufacturer's instructions. Join front and back shoulder seams with rs together. Fold sleeve in half lengthways, rs together and mark centre point. Match centre of sleeve to shoulder seam, sew sleeves in position.

Join side and sleeve seams.

Placing left over right, sew side edges of collar to cast-off stitches on centre front of neck. Sew cast-off edge of collar evenly in place all around neck edge.

Angora Beanie and Fingerless Gloves

This pretty beanie, complete with flower and leaf detail is a perfect match for a pair of fingerless gloves. The yarn used is a luxurious angora and lamb's wool mix and is soft and warm to the touch. Just one ball is all that you will need to make both projects.

✳✳ Intermediate

MEASUREMENTS

To fit 3–5 years

Beanie: Width 46 cm (17–18 in); depth 18 cm (7 in)

Gloves: Length 12 cm (5½ in); width around palm 15 cm (6 in)

TENSION

24st x 26 rows st st = 10 cm (4 in) square worked over st st 4 mm (UK 8 / US 6)

MATERIALS

- 1 x 50 g ball Orkney 50/50 in Periodot (will knit up the hat and gloves)
- Knitting needles size 3.75 and 4 mm (UK 8 and 9 / US 5 and 6)

SPECIAL ABBREVIATIONS

Skpso = Sl1, k1, pass slipped stitch over, to decreae a stitch.

Tip This yarn sheds a little to begin with so knit with a cloth over your knees.

Using 4 mm (UK 8 / US 6) knitting needles, cast on 90 sts.

Knit 1 row.

Row 2: (RS) K1,*k2tog twice, [yfwd, k1] 3 times, yfwd, [skpso] twice, rep from * to last st, k1.

Row 3: Purl

Rows 4 and 5: Knit

These last 4 rows form the pattern and are repeated. Work last 4 rows 8 more times.

Work 2 rows in st st.

Continue in st st and shape crown:

Row 1: *K5, k2tog* to last 6 sts, k6 (78 sts).

Rows 2–4: St st.

Row 5: *K4, k2tog* to last 6 sts, k6 (66 sts)

Rows 6–8: St st.

Row 9: *K3, k2tog* to last st, k1 (53 sts).

Rows 10–12: St st.

Row 13: *K2, k2tog* to last st, k1 (40 sts).

Rows 14–16: St st.

Row 17: *K1, k2tog* to last st, k1 (27 sts).

Row 18: Purl.

Row 19: K2tog across row to last st, k1

(14 sts).

Break yarn, thread through stitches on needle, draw up and fasten off.

FLOWERS

Using 3.75 mm (UK 9 / US 5) knitting needles cast on 14 sts.

Row 1: Purl.

Row 2: Inc in every stitch to end of row.

Row 3: Knit.

Row 4: Cast off 2 sts, *yrn and slip stitch on needle over the yrn, k1, cast off 1*, rep from * to *. Continue casting off in this manner until all stitches are worked. Fasten off. The piece will curl as you cast off. Form the curl into a rose. Secure with a few stitches.

Make 2.

LEAVES

Using 3.75 mm (UK 9 / US 5) knitting needles, cast on 10 sts.

Knit 2 rows.

Row 3: Cast off 6 sts, knit to end.

Row 4: **K4, cast on 6 sts.

Row 5: Knit.

Row 6: Knit.**

Row 7: Cast off 6 sts, knit to end.

Rep from ** to ** and cast off all stitches.

To Make Up

Sew side seam of hat. Seam will run down the back of the head. Attach flowers and leaves to one side of the hat

GLOVES

Using 4 mm (UK 8, US 6) needles cast on 35 sts .

Knit 1 row.

Row 2: (RS) K1, *k2tog twice, [yfwd, k1,] 3 times, yfwd, [skpso] twice , rep from * to last st, k1.

Row 3: Purl

Row 4 and 5: Knit

Rows 2–5 form the pattern. Repeat the pattern twice more.

Work 18 rows st st.

Change to 3.75 mm (UK 9 / US 5) knitting needles.

Work 7 rows garter st. Cast off.

Make two flowers as for hat, but cast on 8 sts instead of 14. Make 2

To Make Up

Sew in ends. Fold glove in half and sew side seam, leaving an opening for thumb. Attach a flower to the back of each glove.

About the Author

Knitting and crochet have been a lifelong passion for Val Pierce. She was taught to knit when she was just 5 years old and progressed from making dolls clothes and scarves to knitting garments for friends and family. Later she checked patterns for knitwear designers and yarn companies, before progressing to become a designer-maker. Val began designing regularly for several magazines and had her first book, *Cutest Ever Baby Knits*, published in 2010. Since then she has written many more knitting and crochet books. Val particularly loves designing for children and babies. She lives and works in Shropshire in the UK.

Index